Cool COUNTRY MUSIC

Create & Appreciate What Makes Music Great!

Mary Lindeen

ABDO Publishing Company

Visit us at www.abdopublishing.com

Published by ABDO Publishing Company, 8000 West 78th Street, Edina, Minnesota 55439. Copyright © 2008 by Abdo Consulting Group, Inc. International copyrights reserved in all countries. No part of this book may be reproduced in any form without written permission from the publisher. The Checkerboard Library™ is a trademark and logo of ABDO Publishing Company.

Printed in the United States.

Design and Production: Mighty Media, Inc.
Photo Credits: Anders Hanson, Photodisc, Shutterstock
Series Editor: Pam Price

Library of Congress Cataloging-in-Publication Data

Lindeen, Mary.
  Cool country music : create & appreciate what makes music great! / Mary Lindeen.
      p. cm. -- (Cool music)
  Includes index.
  ISBN 978-1-59928-970-0
  1. Country music--History and criticism--Juvenile literature. 2. Country music--Instruction and study--Juvenile. I. Title.

  ML3524.L55 2008
  781.642--dc22

                            2007039881

Note to Adult Helpers

Some activities in this book require the help of an adult. An adult should closely monitor any use of a sharp object, such as a utility knife, or perform that task for the child.

Contents

The Music Around You 4

The Country Music Story 6

What Is Country Music? 8

Country Instruments 10

Country Music Legends 12

Music Production and Collection 14

Experience Country Music 16

Make Your Own Banjo 18

Country Music Rhythm 21

Write a Country Song 22

Dance the Texas Two-Step 26

Have a Barn Dance! 28

Conclusion 30

Glossary 31

Web Sites 31

Index 32

The Music Around You

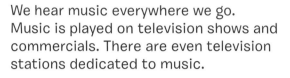

Did you ever get a song stuck in your head? Maybe you just couldn't help singing it out loud. Sometimes a song reminds you of a day with your friends or a fun vacation. Other times a tune may stay in your mind just because you like it so much. Listening to music can be fun and memorable for everyone.

We hear music everywhere we go. Music is played on television shows and commercials. There are even television stations dedicated to music.

Most radio stations play one type, or **genre**, of music. Some play only country music. Others play just classical music. Still others play a mixture of different kinds of rock music. Just pick a kind of music that you like, and you will find a radio station that plays it!

The different genres of music have many things in common, though. They all use instruments. Some instruments are played in many different types of music. The differences are in the ways instruments are played. For example, the drumbeats are different in various music genres.

Some kinds of music have **lyrics** that are sung by singers. Did you know that the human voice is often referred to as an instrument?

Playing music can be as fun as listening to it! Every person can play a part in a song. You can start with something simple, such as a tambourine. You could then work your way up to a more difficult instrument, such as a drum set. Remember, every great musician was once a beginner. It takes practice and time to learn how to play an instrument.

With music, one of the most important things is to have fun! You can dance to it, play it, or listen to it. Find your own musical style and make it your own!

A Mini Musical Glossary

classical music – a type of music from Europe that began centuries ago as the first written church music. Today it includes operas and music played by orchestras.

country music – a style of music that came from the rural parts of the southern United States. It is based on folk, gospel, and blues music.

hip-hop music – a style of music originally from New York City in which someone raps lyrics while a DJ plays or creates an instrumental track.

Latin music – a genre of music that includes several styles of music from Latin America. It is influenced by African, European, and native musical styles. Songs may be sung in Spanish, Portuguese, or Latin-based Creole.

reggae music – a type of music that came from Jamaica in the 1960s. It is based on African and Caribbean music and American rhythm and blues.

rock music – a genre of music that became popular in the 1950s. It is based on country music and rhythm-and-blues styles.

The Country Music Story

A century ago, almost half of the people in the United States lived on farms. Today less than 1 percent of U.S. residents live on farms. Many people have left country life but not country music. It's more popular today than ever.

1940s and 1950s. After World War II, many returning soldiers left the South to find work. They took country music with them to new homes in California and other states. Television was the newest craze. In 1955, one network began broadcasting concerts from the Grand Ole Opry in Nashville, Tennessee. Famous singers such as Bing Crosby and Tony Bennett recorded country songs.

Late 1800s to early 1900s. Country music began in the Appalachian Mountains. The farmers there could barely raise enough food to stay alive. Music was free, and it gave people an escape from their difficult lives. People knew many folk and church songs, which their parents and grandparents brought from Europe. They also made up songs about their hopes, dreams, and hard lives.

1920

1930

1940

1920s. Radio became very popular, and record companies wanted new music to sell. In 1923, a talent scout made the first country music record in Georgia. John Carson sang "The Little Old Log Cabin in the Lane." In 1927, the Carter Family and Jimmie Rodgers made records. Today the Carters are called first family of country music. Rodgers is called the father of country music.

1930s. The nation fell on hard times during the Depression. Businesses failed. People lost their jobs and their homes. People wanted to escape their troubles. They went to the movies, especially westerns starring singing cowboys. As a result, more people became fans of country music.

1960s. Rock music was new and in style. Many singers and bands blended rock-and-roll sounds with country sounds. These musicians, such as Glen Campbell and the Beach Boys, were called crossover artists. Country music and hillbillies were the themes of popular television shows such as *The Beverly Hillbillies* and *Hee Haw*.

1980s. *Urban Cowboy*, starring John Travolta, was a hit movie. Billy Ray Cyrus led the country line-dancing craze. Singers such as Garth Brooks and Barbara Mandrell put on dazzling high-energy shows for crowds of screaming fans. Country music had become as big as rock music.

1990s to today. Country music is still very popular in the United States and around the world. It is also a big business that keeps on growing. One hit song can be worth millions of dollars.

1960

1970

1980

1990

1970s. Country music was big business. Some musicians, including Kenny Rogers and Dolly Parton, made country hits with a smoother pop-music sound. Other country artists thought country music should go back to its roots. Back-to-basics musicians such as Willie Nelson and Waylon Jennings became known as outlaws.

Some people think that country music is too far from its beginnings. Others believe that country music is right where it should be. It is still music about real things that happen to ordinary people. Its sound changes according to the times and the lives of the people who sing it. And that is exactly how it started more than a century ago.

What Is Country Music?

Country music includes many styles based on common elements. Each style has roots in the mountain music of the early 1900s. All of it features down-to-earth songs about the lives and emotions of ordinary people. Sometimes the music is sad, and sometimes the music is funny. But it's all country.

Western Swing

Western swing, or hillbilly jazz, became popular in the 1930s. Bob Wills and His Texas Playboys were among the first western swing bands. This music mixes country sounds with blues, jazz, and big-band swing. The musicians use trombones, drums, and other instruments not commonly used in country music.

Bluegrass

Bill Monroe and His Blue Grass Boys are probably the most famous bluegrass musicians. In fact, the term *bluegrass* was coined to describe the music of this band from the Bluegrass State of Kentucky. This music features fast picking and **strumming** on stringed instruments such as banjo and mandolin. It is also known for close, high-pitched **harmony** singing. Bluegrass musicians prefer **acoustic** instruments.

Honky-tonk

Honky-tonk music became popular in the 1950s. It takes its name from the small-town nightclubs known as honky-tonks. Soldiers returning from World War II went to honky-tonks to forget their troubles. They liked songs about broken hearts, loneliness, and hard living. Hank Williams was their music hero.

Rockabilly and Country Rock

Rockabilly is a cross between country music and blues. It got its start in the 1950s. Country musicians such as Elvis Presley and Jerry Lee Lewis added electric guitars, gospel passion, and boogie-woogie rhythms to their acts. When rock and roll became popular in the 1960s, rockabilly just about disappeared.

Its cousin, country rock, got its start around that same time. It was rock music about down-to-earth topics rather than politics. Gram Parsons, Emmylou Harris, and the Eagles were country rock favorites.

Tex-Mex

Just as its name suggests, Tex-Mex music blends sounds from southern Texas and northern Mexico. Traditional Mexican folk music is combined with Texas rock, country, and blues. Songs are sung in both Spanish and English. Freddy Fender and Los Lobos are well-known Tex-Mex musicians.

Alternative Country

Alternative country, or alt-country, began in the 1990s. It provided a different country music style for fans who were tired of big-name, mainstream country music. Alt-country mixes earlier styles of country music with new rock sounds. Uncle Tupelo, Lucinda Williams, and Kelly Willis are popular alternative country artists.

Country Instruments

Stringed instruments have been at the center of the country music sound since it started. Many modern country bands have drums and electric guitars. But the strings are still the stars in country music!

piano

bass fiddle

guitar

zither

banjo

resonator guitar

mandolin

lap steel guitar

harmonica

fiddle

dulcimer

Inventing Instruments

Country music began in places where people were extremely poor. People often had to make their own instruments. Sometimes they made instruments using whatever they had around their homes. All of these common household items can be used as musical instruments.

Spoons. Hold two spoons together by the handles. Then tap the scoops against each other by striking them against your hand or between your hand and your leg.

Jugs. By blowing across the opening of an empty jug, you can make a whistling sound. Different-sized jugs create different sounds.

Washboards. You play a washboard by rubbing something hard, such as a thimble, across its ridges.

Country Music Legends

Over time, many singers, songwriters, and musicians have made their mark on country music. Listed here are just a few of these famous performers. The songs on page 13 are considered country music classics.

Singers

- Garth Brooks
- Johnny Cash
- Patsy Cline
- Merle Haggard
- Waylon Jennings
- George Jones
- Loretta Lynn
- Willie Nelson
- Dolly Parton
- Jimmie Rodgers
- Hank Williams
- Tammy Wynette

Groups

- Bill Monroe and His Blue Grass Boys
- The Carter Family
- Dixie Chicks
- The Foggy Mountain Boys
- The Judds
- Oak Ridge Boys
- The Statler Brothers

Songs

- "Blue Moon of Kentucky," Bill Monroe and His Blue Grass Boys

- "Crazy," Patsy Cline

- "Friends in Low Places," Garth Brooks

- "Galveston," Glen Campbell

- "He Stopped Loving Her Today," George Jones

- "I Fall to Pieces," Patsy Cline

- "I'm So Lonesome I Could Cry," Hank Williams

- "Mamas Don't Let Your Babies Grow Up to Be Cowboys," Willie Nelson and Waylon Jennings

- "Ring of Fire," Johnny Cash

- "Stand by Your Man," Tammy Wynette

- "Your Cheatin' Heart," Hank Williams

The Life of a Legend

Hank Williams (1923–1953) is perhaps the most important country music singer and songwriter of all time. His career was short. His personal life was a mess. And, he died young. But he wrote many well-known country classics, including these songs.

- "Cold, Cold Heart"

- "Hey, Good Lookin'"

- "Honky Tonk Blues"

- "I'm So Lonesome I Could Cry"

- "Your Cheatin' Heart"

Music Production and Collection

Music Production

The way that music is recorded makes a big difference in its final sound. The type of microphone used and where it is placed are very important. The **acoustics** in the recording room are critical.

Recording music is a difficult process. That is why most country musicians record in recording studios. A recording studio has professional recording equipment. It also has soundproof rooms. Studio engineers place the microphones and run the equipment.

Once the music is recorded, it needs to be worked with to bring out the best sound. This is mostly done with computer programs that help separate the sounds. This process is called mixing.

This sound engineer is using a mixing board.

Downloading Music

At one time, music could be bought only at record stores. Today you can buy music by downloading it onto your computer from a Web site. You can then put the downloaded music onto an MP3 player.

Sometimes people violate **copyright** law when they download music. Copyright law helps musicians get paid for their music. Some illegal Web sites let people download music without paying. You need to make sure you are downloading music from a legal Web site. Otherwise, you could be breaking copyright law.

It is also important that you get permission from an adult before downloading music. When you download music, you are charged a fee. Make sure an adult knows how much the music costs. And make sure an adult knows the Web site you are downloading from.

Record Collecting

Many people collect vinyl records. Music stores sell new and used records. You can also find used records at garage and estate sales. Many **audiophiles** prefer the sound of records. They believe the sound is warmer and truer than the sound of CDs.

Experience Country Music

There are many places country music fans can go to hear their favorite singers and musicians. Here are just a few ways you can experience and learn about country music.

Live Performances

Check out concert listings in the newspaper. These are usually in the entertainment section. You can hear live country music at stadiums, state fairs, music festivals, and local **venues**. Remember that many places require adults to accompany children under the age of 18.

Radio and Television

There are country music radio stations in almost all areas. Wherever you are, you can probably tune in to at least one. There are also country music cable television networks. You can watch music videos and see interviews with famous musicians. You can even hear news about the country music industry.

Libraries

At most libraries, you can check out compact discs just like you check out books. Some libraries also have record albums available. This is often the only way to hear some older country music recordings.

Country Music Museums

A country music museum is the perfect place to learn about the history of country music. It is also where you can learn more about country music stars. Check your newspaper to see if any local museums are featuring exhibits related to country music. Or visit one of these famous country music museums.

Country Music Hall of Fame and Museum

Nashville, TN
www.countrymusichalloffame.com

From flashy costumes to priceless guitars, this museum has tons of country music items. It has video and audio recordings. And, it has interactive computer learning stations.

Grand Ole Opry Museum

Nashville, TN
www.opry.com

This museum showcases the stars who have appeared on the most famous stage in country music. Backstage tours of the Grand Ole Opry House are also available.

Ryman Auditorium

Nashville, TN
www.ryman.com

During the day, you can tour a backstage dressing room. And, you can record your own country music compact disc. At night, live country music concerts are held in this restored auditorium.

Seating at Ryman Auditorium

Make Your Own
BANJO

Materials Needed

- empty one-gallon (3.8 L) plastic bottle, such as a milk or water jug
- marker
- scissors or knife
- 1 small nail
- 1 board about 2 feet × 3 inches × 1/2 inch (61 cm × 8 cm × 1.3 cm)
- hammer
- nylon string or fishing line
- staple gun
- masking or duct tape
- large screw eye

String instruments are the heart and soul of country music. You can make your own banjo using household items and a few simple tools.

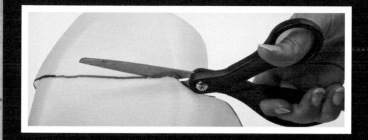

Step 1

Use the marker to draw a line around the plastic bottle, about halfway between the bottom and the top. Use scissors or a knife to cut the bottle in half along the line. Save both parts of the bottle.

Step 2

Center the nail one inch (2.5 cm) from the end of the board. Use the hammer to pound the nail almost all the way into one end of the board. Leave enough room to tie a string around the nail later.

Step 3

Use scissors or a knife to cut two flaps in opposite sides of the bottom half of the jug. The slots should be about a half inch (1.3 cm) from the bottom of the bottle. They need to be about the same width and thickness as the board.

Step 4

To attach the neck to the body, slide the end of the board without the nail through the slots. This end of the board should stick out past the plastic jug only an inch or two (2.5 to 5 cm). The nail should be at the far end, away from the plastic bottle. Staple the plastic flaps to the board to hold the banjo together.

Step 5

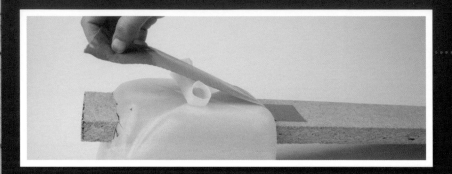

Cut the handle off the top of the plastic bottle. Tape the handle to the middle of the bottom of the bottle. This will make the bridge. The bridge is the bump that raises the strings.

Step 6

Screw the screw eye into the short end of the board that is near the jug. It should be about one inch (2.5 cm) from the end of the board. Screw the screw eye about halfway into the wood.

Step 7

Tie one end of the nylon line to the nail. Pull the string **taut** and wrap the loose end clockwise a few times around the threads of the screw eye. Then pass the end through the eye of the screw and knot it. To change the sound of your banjo, turn the screw eye to tighten or loosen the string.

Country Music RHYTHM

Country musicians often use guitars instead of drums to make the rhythm for their music. **Strumming** a guitar produces a steady beat just like striking a drum.

Step 1

To make a rhythm, clap or tap in sets of three beats or four beats. Clap louder or tap harder on the stressed beat.

Stress the first of three beats to create a waltz rhythm:

1-2-3, **1**-2-3, **1**-2-3, **1**-2-3, etc.

Try stressing the first and third beats of a four-beat rhythm.

1-2-**3**-4, **1**-2-**3**-4, **1**-2-**3**-4, **1**-2-**3**-4, etc.

Listen to how the rhythm changes if you stress the second and fourth beats instead.

1-**2**-3-**4**, 1-**2**-3-**4**, 1-**2**-3-**4**, 1-**2**-3-**4**, etc.

Step 2

Keep trying new rhythms until you find one you like.

CLEF NOTES

Maybelle Carter of the Carter Family invented a way to play both melody and rhythm at the same time on a guitar. She played the melody on the bass strings, or lower sounding strings. She strummed the higher strings to produce the rhythm. This was called the Carter Scratch. It has become one of the most popular ways to play the guitar in country music.

21

Write a
COUNTRY SONG

There's a popular saying in Nashville. And that is, "It all begins with a song."

Country music is all about the songs. It's not about fancy instruments. It's not about flashy shows. It's not about famous stars. Anyone with the right words and the right voice has a chance to make it big in country music.

Materials Needed

- a notebook or a computer
- a tape recorder or a computer with a microphone
- an instrument

Country Lyrics

Country music is all about real life. Songwriters use experiences from their own lives as ideas for their songs. They write about their childhoods. They write about good things that have happened to them. They write about bad things that have happened to them. They write about what they wish would happen to them.

No matter what the topic, a country song has direct, straightforward **lyrics**. Country songwriters tell it like it is. They don't hide their message behind vague phrases and thick symbolism. If a song is about a train, it will say it is about a train. You don't have to figure out that a song about a snake is really about a train. You should say what you mean and mean what you say when you write a country song.

1 First, decide what you want to write about. Start by thinking about a time in your life when you were really happy or really sad. Can you turn that into a good story to tell? Or, think about something you wish would happen to you. If you're stuck, try writing about something or someone you love.

2 Write a rough draft of your lyrics. Don't worry about getting every word exactly right. This is just an outline of your song. This step gives you the "bones" to build your song on.

3 Start writing! Begin by breaking the story down into three or four reasonable chunks. Each chunk of ideas can be a verse of your song. Think about how your song begins and ends. Does it start and stop the way you want it to?

4 Now go back and polish your work. Make sure you've chosen the best words for your song. Make sure you've organized your ideas in the way that is the most satisfying to you.

Country Melody

The melody is the pattern of notes that make up a song. You can come up with a melody by humming something you like. Then figure out how to play that on an instrument.

1 Experiment with patterns of notes until you find something you like. Write it down or record it so that you don't forget it. You might come up with several different melodies you like. Great! Make notes about each one.

2 Now match your melody to the **lyrics** you wrote. You might have to change the words to fit the melody. Or you might have to play with the melody to get it to fit the words. Or you might have to do both. This is the balancing act of songwriting.

3 When you have finally decided what you really like best, write that down or record it. You don't want to forget it. And you want to be able to play it again and again.

Put It Together, Y'All!

1 First, get the rhythm of your music going. Tap your foot on the floor to the beat of your song.

2 Next, play the melody of your song on an instrument. How about using your homemade banjo? Keep practicing. It may take a while before you can play and keep your foot tapping.

3 Now, add the lyrics. Sing the words while you tap the beat and play the notes.

Back in the Saddle Again and Again and Again

It takes a lot of practice to be able to keep a beat, play an instrument, and sing at the same time. Don't worry if it takes a while before you can do this well. Here are some tips for sounding better faster.

Make a recording of your foot tapping the beat. Then play the recording while you play the instrument and sing.

Get some friends to help. Have one person tap the beat. Have another person play the melody. Then you can concentrate on singing.

Make a recording of the beat and the instrument playing the song. Then you can play the recording over and over again while you practice singing.

Dance the Texas
TWO-STEP

Materials Needed

- country music from a CD, a computer file, or the radio
- a large, clear floor to practice on
- a dance partner

No one knows for sure when or where this simple dance started. But it has become one of the most popular kinds of country dancing. The Texas two-step actually has four steps! There are two quick steps and two slow steps. It's kind of like walking, only it's faster and has more style!

Get Ready

1 Face your partner. The leader, usually the boy, puts his right hand on the girl's waist. He holds his left arm up with the elbow slightly bent. His left palm is facing his partner.

2 The girl puts her right arm up. Her right hand rests loosely in the boy's left hand. The girl's left hand is on the boy's right shoulder. Her left arm is slightly bent.

The Steps

1 First, there are two quick steps.

Beat 1. The boy takes a quick step forward with his left foot. At the same time, the girl takes a quick step back with her right foot.

Beat 2. The boy takes a quick step forward with his right foot. At the same time, the girl takes a quick step backward with her left foot.

2 Then, there are two slow steps.

Beat 3. The boy takes a slow step forward with his left foot. The girl takes a slow step backward with her right foot.

Beat 4. Both dancers pause, holding the same positions as in beat 3.

Beat 5. The boy takes a slow step forward with his right foot. At the same time, the girl takes a slow step back with her left foot.

Beat 6. Both dancers pause, holding the same positions as in beat 5.

3 Repeat the steps for beats 1 through 6 as you move to the music.

Remember to slide or shuffle your feet from step to step. Don't pick your feet up too high.

Try not to look down at your feet while you dance. It will only confuse you!

It might help to think "quick, quick, slow, slow" as you dance.

Have a BARN DANCE!

Country music got its start in the mountains long before there were radios, televisions, records, and compact discs. If people wanted to hear music, they had to make their own. Family members played and sang for each other. They performed for audiences made up of sleeping babies and backyard dogs.

From time to time, neighbors would get together at the only place big enough to hold them all, a farmer's barn. There they sat on hay bales and sang and danced together. This was called a barn dance.

In the 1920s, many barn dances were broadcast on the radio. Then radio stations began broadcasting barn dances that weren't really barn dances. They were country music concerts held at hotels and concert halls. A typical barn dance show had

- square dancing
- country, bluegrass, and gospel singers
- string bands
- hillbilly comics
- singing cowboys
- an announcer or an emcee

Host a Hoedown!

1 Plan a short program of country music. Include a song or two that you will sing and some music to dance to. You can even include some jokes about country music or country life. Decide what clothes you and others in the show will wear. Gather any musical instruments, recording equipment, and props you will need.

2 Invite your family and friends to an old-fashioned barn dance. Have some hay bales or sofa cushions and pillows for them to sit on.

3 Have the announcer welcome everyone and introduce the acts. Sing a song or two. Demonstrate a country dance. Then invite the audience to dance to country music. Have someone tell a few country jokes. Have fun re-creating a truly American musical performance!

CLEF NOTES

The most famous radio barn dance is the Grand Ole Opry. It began broadcasting on Saturday nights in December 1925. It got its name in 1927. It happened when switching from a classical music program to the Nashville barn dance program. The announcer said, "For the past hour we have been listening to music taken largely from the Grand Opera, but from now on we will present the Grand Ole Opry."

Conclusion

For 30 years, hopeful country musicians traveled to Nashville. They dreamed of standing at center stage in Ryman Auditorium. It was home to the Grand Ole Opry from 1943 to 1974. To perform at the Opry was proof that you had made it as a country music artist.

Center stage at the Ryman was a symbol of hope for country musicians. So, they took along some of the old floorboards when the Opry moved to a new building. Today country artists still get to perform on that circle of old wood from Ryman. It was installed in the middle of the stage at the new Opry concert hall.

That's a little bit like country music itself. The music keeps growing and changing with the times. It finds room for new artists, new styles, and new fans. But through it all, it has also held on to its roots. Today's country music still echoes the voices, melodies, and sincerity that came from those southern mountains so long ago.

Country music truly has something for everyone. You might love the songs. You might connect with the emotions behind the music. You might appreciate the history of it. You might be fascinated by the twang, the cowboy hats, and the occasional **yodeling**. As long as you come to it with an open mind, you'll find a reason to keep listening to and learning about country music.

Glossary

acoustic – being an instrument that does not need to be amplified.

acoustics – the properties of a room that affect how sound is heard in it.

audiophile – a person who is very enthusiastic about listening to recorded music.

copyright – the legal right to copy, sell, publish, or distribute the work of a writer, musician, or artist.

genre – a category of art, music, or literature.

harmony – a chord created when two or more close musical notes are sung or played together.

lyrics – the words of a song.

strum – to brush the fingertips or a pick over the strings of an instrument, such as a guitar.

taut – tight and having no slack.

venue – a place where specific kinds of events take place.

yodel – to sing in a style that changes rapidly between normal tones and high, false tones.

Web Sites

To learn more about cool music, visit ABDO Publishing Company on the World Wide Web at **www.abdopublishing.com**. Web sites about cool music are featured on our Book Links pages. These links are routinely monitored and updated to provide the most current information available.

Index

A

Acoustics, 14
Alternative country, 9
Audiophiles, 15

B

Banjos, 10, 18-20
Barn dances, 28-29. *See also* Dancing
Beat (of country music), 21
Bluegrass, 8

C

Collecting (country music), 15, 30
Concert venues, 16
Copyright law, 15
Country groups, 12. *See also* Performers
Country Music Hall of Fame and Museum, 17
Country rock, 9
Country songs, 13

D

Dancing (to country *music),* 26-27, 28-29
Downloading music, 15

E

Elements (of country music), 8-9

G

Genres (of music), 4, 5
Grand Ole Opry Museum, 17, 29, 30
Groups. *See* Country groups
Guitars, 10, 21

H

History (of country music), 6-7, 8-9, 17, 30
Honky-tonk, 9

I

Instruments
in country music, 10-11, 25
homemade types of, 18-20
in music, 4, 5
inventing of, 11

L

Listening
to country music, 16, 30
to music, 4, 5
Lyrics (of country music), 23, 24, 25

M

Melody (of country music), 21, 24, 25
Museums (about country music), 17

P

Performers (of country music), 6-7, 8-9, 12, 13
Playing
country music, 24, 25, 28-29, 30
music, 4, 5
Practicing (country *music),* 25
Producing (country music), 14. *See also* Recording

R

Radio stations (for country music), 16
Recording (country music), 14, 17, 24, 25
Rhythm (of country music), 21, 25
Rockabilly, 9
Ryman Auditorium, 17, 30

S

Singers. *See* Performers
Singing, 4
Songs. *See* Country songs
String instruments, 10-11, 18. *See also* Instruments
Styles (of country music), 8-9

T

Television stations (for country music), 16
Tex-Mex, 9
Texas two-step (dance move), 26-27
Types (of music). *See* Genres

W

Western swing, 8
Writing (country *music),* 22-25